this
notebook
belongs to:

Made in the USA
Las Vegas, NV
30 November 2020

11729712R10061